101 Effective Copywriting Techniques

Table Of Contents

Chapter No.		Name	Page No.
		Preface	5
1.		Introduction	8
	a.	All About A Sales Letter	8
	b.	Comparison Between Unsolicited Proposals, Brochures And Sales Letters	10
	c.	Segmentation, Targeting And Positioning	12
	d.	Following The Aida Model	13
2.		Basic Elements Of A Sales Letter	15
	a.	What Are The Basic Parts Of A Sales Letter?	15
	b.	How To Create Headlines To Invigorate Your Sales Letters?	17
	c.	Is It Important To Have A Strong First Paragraph?	19
	d.	Is Including P.S. In Your Sales Letter Essential?	21
	e.	Should You Include Guarantees?	22
3.		Tips On Writing A Sales Letter	25
	a.	Fundamental Tips On How To Write An Effective Sales Letter	25
	b.	A 12-Step Guideline For A Sales Letter	27
	c.	What Fundamental Questions Should Your Sales Letter Answer	33
	d.	Is Aesthetics Important For Your Sales Letter?	35

	e.	Do Short, Powerful Phrases Enhance The Impact Of Your Sales Letter	37
	f.	Why Certain Sales Letters Lose Business	40
	g.	What Are Lethal Sales Letter Mistakes?	43
	h.	What Are The Pitfalls Of A "What If" Approach?	45
	i.	What To Do When You Just Cannot Write A Sales Letter	47
	j.	The Disparity Between A Sales Letter And An Advertisement	49
	k.	Attention Is Critical	50
	l.	A Rapid Lesson In Writing Sales Letters In A Lucid Manner	52
	m.	What Is Better - A Long Or A Short Sales Letter	54
	n.	Do You Always Have To Use Correct English	55
	o.	Monster Of A Sales Letter	56
	p.	Is It True That Good Sales Letters Are Like Good Salespeople	59
	q.	The Ten Basic Rules Of Writing A Good Sales Letter	62
	r.	Five Useful Secrets Of An Effective Sales Letter	64
	s.	Do Emotionally Charged Sales Letters Boost Sales	65
	t.	What Are The Words That You Should Never Make Use Of In A Sales Letter	67
	u.	Ways To Create A Rapport	70
4.		Finishing Up	71
	a.	Final Checklist For A Sales Letter	71

	b.	The Last Word	73

Preface

The basic aim of every business is to enhance stakeholder value. Whether you are keen on generating a huge response from a newspaper or magazine ad, a direct sales letter, or an Internet site, the basic fact you need to realize is "What is it that makes your business tick?"

A chief and extensively used form of marketing communication tool is the sales letter. It can construct your client base and increase your sales.

What is so special about sales letters that are always read? What is it about the sales letters that sell products? What is the secret to sales letters that keep readers reading until the final line? Why do we buy on the basis of some sales letters and not others, even though they offer the same benefits and features?

Sales letters can portray numerous kinds of information. For example:

a) It makes you aware of the product and services that you are offering.
The primary and major reason for using sales letters as a marketing tool is to make the customer conscious of your product or service by providing adequate facts to appeal to the reader.

b) Make an excuse for futures appointment
Sales letter may be used to organize the consumer for contacting in future appointment—for example, visiting him personally or calling him up for appointments.

c) Replying to enquiries.
If at a previous date, the customer asked for additional information about a specific product or service, a sales letter can be sent to respond to their queries. This, in itself, can create ground to sell the product and service.

d) General Information

A sales letter can notify the consumer of the latest offers, products, services, sales, and so on. It can be any other information that you feel will interest the reader. The consumer may have specially asked you to inform him about such information and/or you may target consumer groups exclusively.

To help in establishing how you should write your sales letter, it is important to map out your objectives. Once you are clear about your objective, it will be easy for you to adopt the required technique. Here can be a few of them:

a) For selling any Product or Service
If your sole aim is to sell your products or service, you need to convince people. You need to use words that will convince the prospect of your product or service. Remember, do not be pushy. Talk in a conversational tone.

b) To Notify the Customer
If your sole objective is to provide the consumer with all essential information about your business or product or service? Such sales letters are, as a result, usually escorted with leaflets and other inserts to give such information.

c) To Get a Response
The prospects may contact you for many reasons other than wanting to buy the product or service. It can be for further information, a free sample/trial, a personal visit, etc. Habitually, consumers do not like buying without physically seeing or trying out the product/service. So you must keep an option to demonstrate open. This also helps build credibility. The prospect will feel that you are genuinely interested in them and not just there to sell your products.

Everyone can write a wonderful sales letter. Sure, you may have to study some new skills. Always know, the famous copywriters of today weren't born knowing how to write great sales letters. All of them started from scratch. They also had their initial trouble and failures. But they persisted. In fact, once you know how to play the game, you will yourself realize that writing an effective sales letter is like child's play.

This ebook will take you step by step through the process of writing an effectual sales letter. Starting from what your objective is, to the basic elements of a sales letter, to valuable tips on how to enhance your sales letter to increase sales...you will find everything in this ebook.

Happy Reading.

Chapter 1 - Introduction

(a) All About A Sales Letter

A sales letter is a document intended to generate sales. It influences the reader to place an order, to request for information about a product or service. The basic aim is motivate the reader to take a specific action.

This is a description of a real sales letter.

Results of my R&D
"I'm taking to you to inform you about the really terrific washing machine that I've developed. First of all, I know it's wonderfully terrific because I spent years studying washing machines of all kinds. I then expanded my field of research and Development (R&D) to include all kinds of commercial washing machines, and I came to know about all the possible secrets of what makes dirt come out from the most inconceivable places. Now, TEN YEARS LATER, I'm ready to let you savor the fruits of all my hard work. I've developed the EZ WASHER. I must tell you it will make all other washing machines you have ever seen pale in contrast."

Do you find anything wrong with this sales letter? Almost everything is wrong.

The headline is all about the writer and does not speak to the customer. Also, it uses some technical terms — "R&D" for research and development. This is an industrial term, which may actually irritate some prospective customers. We have no idea whatsoever what the 10 years of work refers to. Neither are we told about any exceptional features. The writer just generally raves about what great work he has done. The sales letter talks about all what he has done in the last 10 years and not what I will get or at least what I can expect.

Before starting to write a sales letter, you must also try to put yourself in the prospective customer's shoes. Realize how you treat unwanted letters that you receive. Most of these letters, if not all, go in the bin. In fact, you don't even bother to open some of them.

(b) Comparison Between Unsolicited Proposals, Brochures And Sales Letters

Whether you are preparing a brochure, or writing an unsolicited proposal, you can always make it better by realizing the similarities and differences between them.

A brochure is a record of your products and services. They are often produced in a large scale and given incognito. Brochures come in different kinds of shapes and sizes and are more often than not printed in bright colors with lots of graphics in it.

An unsolicited proposal is an article about your products and services. They are usually produced independently and given to someone precise (although it may be to someone you are not too familiar with). They are often in the form of a letter, unless they are large documents, which are bound.

A sales letter is a short proposal and always aims towards making you take some action. Depending on the situation, sales letters may or may not be given to precise individuals and are sometimes sent to people you don't know.

So what's the dissimilarity? It turns out that in reality there is not a lot of difference between them. All of them have to offer information and usually seek to influence. Sometimes, the main intention of a brochure is to provide information. A key differentiator is whether the brochure should aim towards making you take some action. Marketing materials are almost always fashioned to stimulate the reader to do something. It could be to visit their store, make a purchase, visit a website, or maybe just to place a telephone call. If your brochure simply supplies information, you should reconsider it to make sure it is convincing, and consider re-designing it to induce people to take an action.

If do you have a call to action, or something that you are trying to inspire the prospective customer to do, then it may help to imagine your brochure to be an unsolicited proposal. The brochure should be intended to efficiently convince the reader to execute the call to action.

If you are writing a sales letter, you may not comprehend that it's not much different than a brochure asking the reader to take action. Try to focus on the aesthetics of the brochure.

Both brochures and unsolicited proposals are liable to suffer from not having too much information about the reader. The more you are familiar with the reader, the more persuasive you can be. However, brochures and unsolicited proposals are frequently given to people who you are not too familiar with, usually in the anticipation of getting to know them better.

The next time you are creating a brochure, unsolicited proposal, or a sales letter, take the time to think over it as if it was one of the others. Utilize the comparison to enhance the document, but be obvious about your goals and audience.

(c) Segmentation, Targeting And Positioning

Preparing your sales letter means you need to really have a comprehensive knowledge of the product or service being offered, the market dynamics, and the reader's stated and unstated needs. There is no replacement for product or service knowledge.

What does the product or service do for the one who requires it? How can the reader benefit from buying it? What is the unique selling point of the product or service? To respond to these queries, you should begin by distinguishing the benefits from the features. The sales letter should be able to persuade your reader to buy your stuff based on the grounds of what benefit the product/service derives and not based on its features.

The benefit is what the product or service offers and what the consumer profits from the feature. A benefit is the specific result of the feature. A feature is what the product or service already has built in. Benefits are what inspire people to buy. A refrigerator, for example, has defrosting facilities (feature). If that technology helps in getting rid of unwanted icicles and helps in keeping our greens fresh and healthy, then we have the benefit of that feature.

Decide on how you plan to advertise the product or service. Through the Internet, direct mail, email, direct sales, print advertising, etc.? Is there some other advertising or literature to support the sales letter? Who is your competition? What marketing activities have they undertaken? What is your advertising budget? Are you aiming too high?

Who is your potential buyer? What stimulates a person to buy this item? The experts point out that the emotion most often used to influence people to buy is fear, and a million other variations of it. You have to be in the consumer's position to realize whether your offer appeals to the readers' emotional needs.

(d) Following The Aida Model

Advertising copywriters follows the AIDA model. The AIDA model stands for **Attention, Interest, Desire, and Action.**

Get Your Reader's Attention
If you want your sales letter to have an impact on your readers, it must first get their attention. You can do this with a hard-hitting headline or lead paragraph that hits the nail directly on the head or you can even begin your letter with a captivating question. For instance, "Do you want to cut your electricity cost by 45%?"

An appropriate headline for a sales letter promoting a weight loss program might be: "Now, you can lose 15 pounds in 2 weeks without having to starve; and it's easy and affordable!" This headline not only solves a problem, but also offers a quick and easy solution that keeps in mind the price-sensitive consumer.

Your reader will be interested only in knowing "What's in it for me?" "Why should I invest my time in reading on?" If you let him know instantly, at the beginning of your letter, he'll keep reading the rest of the letter. And that's half the battle won. In any case, he will rarely reach the third paragraph. So the impact has to be instant. The crux of the matter should be explained at the very beginning.

Gain Their Interest
You must clasp the reader's interest by showing him why he needs your product or service. You have to create a want for your product or service. Let him know how his life will become easier with your product. Show him what he is missing by not even trying the product.

Here, you require to prove your trustworthiness. You can rest your case by using testimonials or case histories. You can provide the communication details of users who have benefited from your product. Always remember that you know everything there is to know about your product, so "stale news" to you can be "fresh news" to the other person.

Create Desire

Now you've got the reader's attention and hooked his interest. Next, you've got to create desire. Tell the reader how exactly he'll benefit from your product. Link the benefits to the reader's daily life. Get him to realize how your product can benefit him, how convenient it is for him to get it, and how comfortable life will be for him afterwards.

Generalities are less convincing. Specific details are far more believable. For example, when you want to sell books on lowering employee theft . . . "By the end of this quarter, you could see your percentage of employee theft drop by more than 37%. Imagine the spectacular effect it will have on your bottom line!" If it is selling a weight loss program... "Within 3 weeks you will have lost 15 pounds. Imagine the compliments pouring in from your spouse. Think how gorgeous you will look in that new swimsuit!"

Solicit Action

What do you want the reader to do next? Send in a reply card? Order the product or service? Call in asking for more information? Schedule an appointment? Notify him accordingly. It is amazing how many sales letters do not inform the reader about the subsequent step. They consider that the reader is a mind reader. But usually this is not the case.

You've worked hard so far. You've gotten his attention, hooked his interest, created desire. Isn't it appropriate to ask for action? Don't presume that your reader knows what to do next. As a support to getting the preferred action, you must always incorporate a reply card with your letter.

The P.S. is one component of a letter that at all times gets read. Use your P.S. to emphasize your most compelling benefit or restate your guarantee. Don't waste it on merriment. Used wisely, it could be the final prod that tilts the buying decision in your favor. So be specific and give the final spurt.

Chapter2 - Basic Elements Of A Sales Letter

(a) What Are The Basic Parts Of A Sales Letter?

Any sales letter roughly follows the following sequence:

a. Image.
b. Headline.
c. Greeting.
d. Lead paragraph.
e. Body.
f. Closing.

The Image:
If there is a logo or design for your business, use it in the sales letter only if it is really pertinent to what you are offering. You are not selling your business logo; you are selling benefits that the buyer will realize if he buys your product or service. Use a specific image that is inherent to your headline, content, and theme, or do not use one at all. Stick to words as far as possible.

Job Of The Headline:
The headline is usually 3 - 30 words long. It should be catchy. It should grab the reader's attention and tell him what the ad (sales letter) is about. Ideally, the job of the headline is to get the reader's concentration, target the viewers, list an advantage, and make an assurance.

Greeting And Lead Paragraph:
Any sales letter that influence the reader has a possibility of being opened and read.
- Spin a yarn that the reader can identify with, using a conversational tone.
- Announce a new product or service, an exclusive event, or important news, flaunting your unique selling proposition.

- Speak to the reader as your equal: "Dear fellow car purchaser, are you aware of. . . "
- You could start with something innovative, perhaps a quote or anecdote.
- You could start by identifying the reader's problem, one that your product promises to solve.
- Ask a question that might excite the reader.
- Let the reader in on some secret or uncommon information.

You could use a sub-headline to answer a query posed in the headline. For example, Part A could say: "Want to lose 15 pounds within 3 weeks at an affordable price?" Part 2 could say: "Well, this is how you can do it . . . "

Body Of The Letter:
The body copy should use the same tone and endure with the theme of the headline. You should persist highlighting the benefits and offer proof of the claim you made. Provide details of the benefits and the features. Build credibility. Your basic objective is to create a need or want for your products or services and make people do what you want them to.

Closing Or Call To Action:
If you solicit the reader to order, support, or to contact you for the particular cause, you must make it easy for him to reply. You must support the sales letter with a prepaid envelope and an order form. If not suitable, supply a toll-free telephone number, an email link, and/or your URL. Always thank the reader for his patience. Always use a postscript.

A Final Suggestion:
Getting the reader to spend his hard-earned money on you is the real challenge. The best way to ensure this is to use test readers. Test readers would be able to give their opinion if anything is missing in the letter.

(b) How To Create Headlines To Invigorate Your Sales Letters?

Every one of your marketing tools would require a headline. Headlines draw attention, make your message simple to read, get your key selling points across, and prompt your customer to buy the product and service.

Use headlines regularly in your sales letter to help people get your main message without having to grope about too much.

Headlines range from "hit-you-in-the face" to more understated ones that don't appear like a headline at all.

Your headline gets noticed when it appeals to the reader's interests. You must use your headline to point out a difficulty the reader has or something you know the reader feels powerfully about.

Seven Sure-Fire Headlines

a. **Ask a Question.** "Are you worried about becoming fat and flabby?" A question headline forces the reader to answer in her mind. You mechanically get the prospect involved in your message.

b. **Begin your headline with "How to."** "How to lose 15 pounds in 3 weeks." People love information that illustrates how to do something valuable.

c. **Provide a testimonial.** The advice of a satisfied customer can act as a catalyst in pursuing others to buy from you.

d. **Issue a command.** Some traditional headlines order readers to "Aim High" and "Move Ahead" and so on. Turn your most significant benefit into a strong headline.

e. **Significant news makes a good headline**. This especially works well for huge changes in your organization or the introduction of savvy new products.

f. **Headline a last date for a special offer**. Most of us are always too busy and tend to put off taking action. "Save Money Now" and "Get Bonus If You Buy Now" offer augment response.

g. **FREE offers often draw the greatest response**. There is a myth that wealthy or professional customers are turned off by free offers. This is not accurate at all. Just customize your free offer so as to match the style of your customers or industry.

Prospects are always hard-pressed for time. They are barraged with hundreds of ads, sales letters, postcards, and commercials every day. They tend to tune out any advertising message that looks like it will take quite long to figure out. Headlines help them decide. So focus on them.

(c) Is It Important To Have A Strong First Paragraph?

The next crucial question is how do you begin your sales letter.
Do you tell the prospective client immediately what it is you're intending to sell? Do you just stir him up a bit so he can comprehend why he would require your product or service?

The course of the initial paragraph of your sales letter depends on the theme you've chosen. That subject will dictate whether your lead paragraph will follow a specific creative approach or focus on your offer.

Once your initial paragraph is at par with your theme, the focal point should shift to your warm-up. An inefficient warm-up will paralyze a sales letter more than any other aspect, resulting in an average letter.

A great sales piece will get to the point instantly. Your objective is to command and draw the interest of the reader. It is not to establish the groundwork for comprehending the piece; it's to create immediate interest in the topic that you have selected.

Also, the initial paragraph should be in the first person. A speedy way to obliterate a letter is to talk in the third person or to include 'we' in the letter. To begin a letter with "we" can spoil your response.

Here is a comprehensive set of the rules to follow in creating your first paragraph:

    a. Make it theatrical, interesting and directed to the exact target audience.
    b. Keep your paragraph concise.
    c. Keep your sentences precise.
    d. Keep your words short.
    e. Use "you" to engage the prospect.
    f. Make your message come from a single person, on a very individual basis, with the aim of building a one-on-one readership throughout the piece.

g. In assessing any sales letter, one of the basic things you should do is examine the lead paragraph. Does it match the approach and taste of the six points listed above?

There is no rigid formula to a lead-in paragraph, but your letters will create enhanced responses if you follow, rather than break, the rules.

(d) Is Including a P.S. In Your Sales Letter Essential?

People do like to know who has sent them the letter, and tend to quickly scroll down to the end of the letter to see whose signature is at the bottom.

The next thing they see below the signature is a Postscript (or P.S.). Truly enough, your P.S. can be the second (after the headline) or third (after the opening sentence/paragraph) most read element of your sales letter or email. Most copywriters use not just one postscript, but also several (P.P.S).

Most postscripts tend to be fairly small, usually about 3 or 4 lines to sum up the offer, corroborate the deadline, and comprise the call for action.

Webster's defines PS.. this way... (verbatim)
"Postscript -- To write after; a paragraph added to a letter after it is concluded and signed by the writer; an addition made to a letter or composition after the main body of the work has been finished, containing something omitted, or something new occurring to the writer."

For marketers, it provides one final opportunity to influence prospects into action. The best way to use your final "addition" is to highlight or re-state a chief point of significance to the reader.

Employ these tactics. The P.S. is one of the most-read elements of any sales letter. It ranks second only to your headline and sub-heads in terms of readership priority.

Keep it concise and precise. A succinct summary is sufficient to uphold the reader's interest. If you need more room, create a secondary P.S. Adding supplementary P.S.'s is a mainly effective strategy with longer sales letters.

(e) Should You Include Guarantees?

If you offer a product or service without a guarantee, you might just be on the verge of losing a great percentage of potential sales. Nowadays, scams are widespread. Since there is no official police or moderator on the Internet, such scams are most likely even greater as a consequence.

Because of these swindlers and the huge number of challenges presented on the Web, people are mistrustful and will increasingly seek out more protected means to advantage from offers. Guarantees are, therefore, influential tools for the opulence-seeking marketer and can do two very vital things that will help grow one's profits: Increase sales and reduce returns.

When you offer a guarantee, you diminish the cynicism around the purchase of your product or service. Consumers are reasonably careful and all the more when making purchases via the Web. And guarantees give you an almost immediate trustworthiness with possible customers.

Guarantees increase perceived value. Take for instance the story of the Monaghan brothers.

Both the brothers were into a home base business. They required money to pay through college. They worked in shifts and attended college when they were free in the other shift. After going through loss for about one year, one of the brothers sold his share in the business. The other stuck to the small pizzeria. In some interviews he recently gave, Tom Monaghan said that, he was not too sure that he was doing the right thing. And rest is history. His decision was the best one he ever made. His business based on a simple guarantee, "Pizza delivered fresh in 30 minutes or it's free," Domino's Pizza became the billion dollar industry of today.

Guarantees increase sales and reduce returns. While people order, particularly from the Web because of the expediency it offers, an offer that provides a no harassment return policy adds to the expediency factor and instills a greater self-assurance in the buyer's mind. So use guarantees to guarantee your success.

Seven Tips for a Grand Guarantee

- Make the guarantee easy and unqualified. Drop the excuses and fine print.

- Be sure your total organization believes in the operating philosophy dictated by the use of guarantees.

- Be familiar with your clients enough to realize whether the guarantee at all helps the client.

- A guarantee should be a two-way road, so include some upside if you surpass performance potential: ask for "success" fees.

- Indicate which clients can claim the guarantee and which cannot. Restrict the number to minimum.

- React quickly if a client requests that you make good on your guarantee.

- Monitor your performance to save surprises.

Guarantees fall into five very different categories:

- The Money-back guarantee: This guarantees that your customers won't squander their time or money. It also defends customers if the product breaks or fails.

- The Satisfaction guarantee: This guarantees that your customer will be happy and satisfied with your service or product.

- Price protection guarantee: This can either offer a fixed price, ensuring the price and/or payment terms won't change or increase (for example, life insurance) or ensure that they won't find a lower price elsewhere.

- On-time guarantee: This helps suppress the fears in time-crunched clientele. Businesses like printers, car repair shops, and cable companies can find such an offer tempting.

- Absolutely No Questions Asked guarantee: This can be functional towards anything. Just try it out and see.

Chapter 3 - Tips On Writing A Sales Letter

(a) Fundamental Tips On How To Write An Effective Sales Letter.

a. **Build Credibility.** Besides mentioning the benefits, you should also put in testimonials of people who have already used and benefited from your product or service. This builds credibility.

b. **Make It Memorable For Your Reader.** Most unsolicited mails get tucked into the dustbin. Your mailer should have something unique for people to consider spending more time on it. For example, a car repair service might include the top 10 tips for car maintenance and so on.

c. **Emphasize Aesthetics.** The letter should be user-friendly. It should have attractive visual impact. The aesthetics should be well defined. Also, it should be easily navigable.

d. **Include A Call To Action.** Include a postcard, prepaid envelope and/or an order form. If not appropriate, supply a toll-free telephone number, an email link, and/or your URL.

e. **Always Include An Enticement.** The letter should include an incentive for acting promptly - a discount, special offer, gifts, and so on.

f. **Resist Doing "Mail Merge."** Technology has made life easier no doubt. But try to avoid writing mass mailers. Customize each letter according to the needs of the reader.

g. **Forge Everlasting Connections.** Try and forge everlasting relations with your customers. For this you have to "under-promise" and "over-deliver."

h. **Test Market**. Whatever technique you intend to apply, always test the market.

i. **Hit The Right Chord**. Your sales letter should not be too formal and full of jargon. That might inhibit the reader.

j. **One Final Tip**: Before sending out the mailers, make sure you have calculated all aspects. You would certainly not want to be flooded with offers without having the appropriate resources.

(b) A 12-Step Guideline For A Good Sales Letter

You don't require being an award-winning copywriter to create proficient sales letters. In reality, writing great sales letters is more scientifically inclined than being an art. Even the professionals use proven "templates" to generate sales letters that get the desired outcome.

Every individual has some form of buying resistance. The basic objective of your sales letter should be to triumph over your reader's buying resistance while coaxing him to take action. These hurdles are noticeable in many stated and unstated customer comments such as:

"You don't realize my real problem" "How do I know you're competent?" "I do not believe you at all" "I don't need it at present" "It won't help me in any way" "What happens if I don't find it useful?" "I can't afford to buy it" and so on.

The sales letter must play on the reader's emotions to the extent where they would be inspired enough to take action. The letter should try to attack those "hot buttons" or emotional pressure points, which will persuade the reader to buy. The two main motivating factors are the promise of gain and the fear of loss.

Would you rather buy a $60 course on "How to Enhance Your Career" or "How to Prevent being handed the Pink Slip?"

Any day, the second title will sell better. Why? Because it addresses the fear of loss.

The following is a 12-step model for writing foolproof sales letters.

Try to Get Attention:
Presuming the reader has opened your envelope; the next important step is to get his attention. The headline is the foremost thing that your reader will

notice. People have a very limited attention span and usually shove their mail into the wastebasket unless the headline jumps out to them.

The following are three examples of headline templates that are proven to get concentration.

HOW TO _____"

THE ESSENTIAL SECRETS OF _____ DISCOVERED!"

WARNING: DON'T EVEN DARE TO _____ UNTIL YOU _____.

Identify the Reader's Problem: Now that the reader has given you her full attention, you have to go straight to the problem area. Try to empathize with the reader.

Another method is to agitate the problem. You present the problem, then excite it so that she really feels the pain and anguish of her situation. People are such sturdy creatures of custom that we hardly bother to change our ways unless we feel immense amounts of pain. In fact, companies are not diverse. Most businesses drag along doing the same old thing until things become so worse that they have to make an alteration.

Provide the Solution to the Problem: Now that you have identified the reader's problem, you become the "savior" by providing her with the solution to the problem. You introduce your product or service and show her how all her problems will vanish once she gets your product/service.

Present your Credentials to the Prospect: Just telling the reader that you can make her life more comfortable and convenient will not prod her to jump in and grab your stuff. You need to build trust and prove your credibility. You can do this in the following manner:

- Listing successful case studies and instances.

- Naming prestigious companies (or people) you have done business with.

- Mentioning your work experience.

- Showing important awards and accolades that you have won.

Show the Benefits of your Products: Now you need to tell the reader how she will personally benefit from your product or service. Don't just mention the features. Nobody is interested in just the features. What you can do instead is, you can draw two columns. In one column, you can write the features and in the other, mention any conceivable benefit that they can receive from the feature. You can also use bullet points for each benefit to make it user-friendly to navigate.

Give Your Social Proof: After you've presented all your benefits, now you need to build your credibility and trust with your reader with testimonials from contented customers.

Testimonials are influential selling tools that establish your claims to be true. Another way of making your testimonial even more influential, include pictures of your customers with their names, addresses, and phone numbers. Most readers won't call to find out. But if you include the numbers, it lends you greater credibility.

Make Your Final Offer: Your offer is the most essential element of your sales letter. If your offer is great, even a mediocre sales copy will make it irresistible.

Your offer can come in many different layouts. The best offers are usually an attractive blend of price, terms, and free gifts. It is always more lucrative to add more and more benefits to your offer rather then just lowering the price.

Give a Promise or Guarantee: You can make your offer even more appealing by taking out the risk factor from it. Remember that people have a built-in fear that marketers are out there to cheat them.

Give a very strong guarantee, but only if you have enough confidence in your product or service. If you provide a guarantee and later do not abide by it, your credibility is shattered. So be careful. If your product or service is good enough, very few people will actually need any refund.

Inject the Elements of Scarcity: Most people take their own sweet time responding to offers, even when they are appealing. There can be many reasons for it, like:

- They don't feel enough discomfort to make a change.
- They are too busy and eventually forget.
- They don't believe that the perceived value justifies the price asked for.
- They are just plain lazy.

To stimulate people to take action, you need to add incentives to the offer. You can create a sense of scarcity by informing your reader that either the supply or the quantity is limited. You can also mention that your offer is valid for only a limited time period.

Your offer could say something like this:

"If you purchase by (so-and-so date) you will get a whole bunch of free gifts."
Or
Our supply is limited to only 60 (product or service) and you will receive it on a "first come, first served" basis. After they are exhausted, there won't be any more available."
Or
"This price is valid only for the next 15 days."

But once you have made such an offer, you cannot go back on it and keep extending the last date. This will make your customers lose confidence in you.

Call to action: Do not presume that your reader is familiar with what to do to obtain the benefits from your offer. You must guide them carefully on how to make the order in very comprehensible and concise language. Tell them whether you want them to call you, fax you, or click the order button on your website

Give a Warning:
A good sales letter should persist to build emotion, even after your call to action.

You can use the "risk of loss" strategy to let the reader know what would happen if they did not take advantage of your existing offer. Maybe they would continue to:

Struggle forever:
- Lose the chance to receive all your valuable goodies.
- No improvement in life.
- See their competitors benefit and rise in life.

Try to paint a sad picture in the psyche of the reader about the penalty of not taking action now. Drill into them how much they are missing out at present.

Close with a Proper Reminder:
You should always include a postscript (P.S.). In your postscript, you might want to remind them of your enticing offer. If you've used scarcity in your sales letter, include your call to action, then remind them of the restricted time (or quantity) offer.

Using this 12-step formula, anyone can write an efficient sales letter that sells.

The following are a few extra tips to help you write an even better sales letter:

Tip 1: Always Mention the Features/Benefits - The biggest obstacle to writing a brilliant sales letter is just getting started. Take a pen and paper and list all the features of your product or service. Then take another paper and list the benefits that can be derived from your product or service.

Tip 2: Once you are done with the letter, forget about it for a day or two. This will allow you to be more practical when you edit your letter.

Tip 3: Develop a "swipe file" to enhance your creativity. When you see a well-executed ad or website sales letter or receive a really effective letter in the mail or email, keep it in a file or folder that you can refer back to again and again. Keep comparing ideas.

Tip 4: Before you start writing your sales letter, create a customer profile sheet by recording every thing you know about your target customer.

Tip 5: Keep your sales letter as lengthy as it needs to be. You can make it a short 2-page article or a 50-page ebook. The essential purpose of both is to inject emotion and prompt action.

(c) What Fundamental Questions Should Your Sales Letter Answer?

Who Are Your Prospective Customers?
Before writing your sales letter, you must target your customer group. You should know whom you want to sell your product or service to. If you were offering a golf stick designed to play golf, you wouldn't market it to men in general. You'd taper it down to people that played. You have to be very specific.

How Is Your Product or Service Differentiated?
What makes your product different from the competition? Have you undertaken a comparative study? If there is anything unique about the product, then flaunt it to the readers.

Why Should The Prospect Have Faith?
With all the scams and fake information being given through advertising, skepticism sets in pretty fast. So you need to make your prospect consider what you're telling them is the irrefutable truth. Build your credibility by offering statistics and testimonials.

What Are All The Benefits Your Product or Service Offers To The Consumer?
List all the visible and not so visible benefits that make your product irresistible to not accept.

Why Might Your Prospect Reject Your Offer?
Walk a mile in the shoes of your prospective buyer. This way you will know what reservations or objections he may have. Once you know it, work on it and resolve the queries.

Why Should Your Prospect Act Now?
The ending question you must reply for your prospect is why he needs to act without more ado. Give him an authentic motive to act instantly. Give him a special price if he acts within the next few days. Or tell him quantities are

restricted and once the stock is exhausted they won't be sold at the same price. Just make sure that your exigency is credible.

(d) Is Aesthetics Important For Your Sales Letter?

Does appearance matter to you? Like most people—including your customers and prospects—your answer is "Yes." Predominantly in sales, appearance is essential. For example, in a competitive situation, all else being equal, the look of the salesperson can be the deciding factor in who closes the deal.

Appearance is also crucial to the success of your sales letter.

The marketer with an extremely targeted mailing list, a strong offer, and successful copy —and who pays cautious attention to how his letter looks — will definitely get more offers than the person who focuses only on content, with no regard to aesthetics. The catchier it is, the better.

Tips on how to make a sales letter look good:

Tip 1: Always use a reader-friendly font. Almost all newspapers and news magazines use serifed fonts for mostly all of their editorial content. Fonts like Times Roman, Courier, and Century are far more readable than fonts like Arial, Helvetica.

Tip 2: Make your headline a catchy one. You must also keep your opening paragraph to between one and three lines.

Tip 3: Try to restrict the length of all your paragraphs to between 4 and 6 lines. Your letter should have an inviting, reader friendly look. Your prospect will definitely not be too happy to see plump, 9 - 11-sentence paragraphs.

Tip 4: Vary the length of your paragraphs so that it does not become too mundane.

Tip 5: Set the body copy of your letter in 10-11 point type and use sub-heads, bullets and other devices to attract attention. Always consider the audience you are writing to. If you're writing for the 20-something crowd, you can most likely even use 10-point type. On the other hand, if you're targeting the "grown-up" market, you may want to use a 14-point font type. Centered, emboldened sub-heads and other eye attracting devices can enhance readership.

Sub-heads, bulleted lists, emboldening, and other devices will give your letter added appeal and augment response. But take care to use these devices carefully. Overuse of them can counteract their overall efficacy.

Using these 5 tips will attract more eyes, make people read for a longer time, create more leads, and, ultimately, close more sales.

Always remember that your letter will be contending with perhaps tens of other sales letters received every day, sent by sales-people vying for attention. To cut through the clutter, your sales letter needs to be excellent, diverse, proficient, and relevant.

(e) Do Short Powerful Phrases Enhance The Impact Of Your Sales Letter?

A slogan is a "noun, usually repeated and persuasive that creates a memorable catch phrase, motto, or jingle, that expresses a particular aim or concept. A concept that you want to stick in your audience's mind like glue to paper."

What makes a slogan unforgettable? Conciseness is first aspect to consider—normally 10 words or less. The slogan should follow a particular rhythm.

Third, what are the benefits for using slogans? Brevity, as mentioned earlier, meets the requirements of today's fast pace. Slogans also manipulate decisions, persuade, and add trustworthiness. A slogan usually makes it easier for the prospect to remember and identify a product or service.

Simple powerful phrases motivate your customer's feelings and generate an emotional decision to buy from you. You can augment your sales by using powerful phrases in your sales letters.

A powerful phrase helps your customer envisage how he will feel when he owns your product or uses your service. It creates an imagined feeling and motivates your customer to translate that feeling into reality. Power phrases increase a customer's longing for your product or service and cause an emotional decision to buy.

Creating a power phrase is simple. Start by recording some of the main benefits your customers receive when they decide to buy from you. Then merge a few highly expressive action words about one or more of those benefits into a short phrase.

Given below are some examples of power phrases used by different types of businesses:

"Quick! Simple! Affordable!"

"I assure you immediate result on my product."

Look at the words used in the above two power phrases. Power phrases use effective words to create forceful statements.

Most effective power phrases usually unite 3 words or 3 groups of words together in a series. Take for example:

"Save time. Save money. Save Hassle."
"Quick! Simple! Affordable!"

"Enjoy it while at home, in the office or in your car"
"Authority, Performance and Momentum"

There are five major slogan types:
- **A feature**: an exclusivity or difference between a substance, product or object. Example: "Write an ebook in 10 days."
- **A benefit**: a result that someone receives. Remember, this saves you [time or money].
- **A query**: thought-provoking methods. "How would you like to earn without having to invest a single penny?"
- **A challenge**: a dare. Example: The Marines, "We are only looking for a few exceptional men."
- **A structure**: a design that might be put together for a particular purpose.

There are seven ways to make a slogan memorable:
- Make it thrilling
- Be arrogant
- Self-referencing
- Figurative, playful or humorous
- Inspirational or motivational
- To generate painful memories
- Use of dramatic language

Life slogans help invigorate goals, dreams, and even change beliefs. In business, slogans are usually used for introducing self, prospective presentations, on websites, in e-mail signatures, and even at speaking engagements. Be imaginative, use a slogan in each of your sales and marketing processes, and change them regularly if you need to.

Where do you start to build slogans? Read through any of your notes or material. Emphasize phrases that contain high energy. Rhyme helps create outstanding slogans. Read poetry for cues or language that influences or inspires.

(f) Why Certain Sales Letters Lose Business

Any advisor can tell you there are numerous methods to lose a sale even when you are confident of winning it. More often than not, the loophole remains in the sales letter itself. Most sellers drool when clients ask for tenders. After all, it's exhilarating to have a prospect to demonstrate your stuff, to win him over, and then close the deal. But creating an impressive proposal is not at all easy, and the process will require immense time and energy.

Illustrated below are a few of the reasons why a sales letter loses sales and how to avoid it

1. Do Not Play the Solitary Steward
Some people conduct rigorous research on the client and the project, thinking that is more than enough. Then they sit to create their proposal in isolation. That is a grave mistake. You cannot simply create a proposal unless the client is an active member in every stage of the proposal process, including research, objectives, potential benefits, scope, approach, and, so on.

2. Do Not Start With Your Qualifications
Do not begin your proposal with the magnificent history of your firm. Your clients are interested in what you can actually do for them. Start your lead paragraph focusing on their program and not how great you are.

3. Do Not Neglect The Executive Synopsis
Many decision-makers are bothered about basically two objects: the executive summary and the price. Yet, surprisingly, some sellers don't include executive summaries in their sales letters. Decision-makers rely on the executive summary to make certain you comprehend what they are trying to accomplish. If you omit the executive summary, you can be very sure your letter will be snugly fitted in the waste paper basket.

4. Do Not Focus Only On Your Tools
Clients care about only the outcome, not the tools, methods and approaches you'll use to reach the result. Do not jabber on about how you want to do this and do that. Tell them what you can do and how soon. The "how" can be discussed later on, once you have managed to bag the project.

5. Keep It Short And Sweet
Research shows that, given a choice, clients consider a shorter proposal before they get lost in a long windy sales letter stuffed with graphics and boilerplate. Keep your proposals as concise as possible, but you must ensure that you meet the requirement of your clients.

6. Do Not Use The Same Resume
Every situation is in some way different from the other. So you cannot present the same resume to everyone. Prepare different templates. Customize your resume for each client. Let them know what varied experiences you have.

7. Do Not Load Your Proposal With Jargon
Most sales letters are full of jargon and technical-sounding words. Such flowery language may be suitable for textbooks, but it usually turns off the client. Try to use simple and informative language.

8. Do Not Cut And Paste
To save time, certain companies believe in the cut-and-paste syndrome. And what is the result? The client receives the proposal of one company with the name of address of another, or vice versa. Make sure you go over the sales letter intricately before mailing it to the client or uploading it to your website. Save the embarrassment.

9. Be Punctual
Do not try to bluff your clients. If you have missed the deadline to submit the sales proposal, be truthful and ask for an extension. Do not try to give inane excuses.

A brilliant proposal can be crucial in being rewarded a project; a poor one can cause you to blow it, even if other things involved in the sales process has gone perfectly. So try to avoid the basic flaws mentioned above.

(g) What Are Lethal Sales Letter Mistakes?

For you to be successful, the prospect must open, read, believe, and act on your sales letter. In order to do this, it has to draw interest and generate a craving for your product or service.

A successful sales letter is supposed to achieve the same result as a successful salesperson. Similarly, like a salesperson, the sales letter will also want to avoid certain mistakes.

Here are a few lethal mistakes, which most sales letters make.

Lethal Sales Letter Mistake # 1 - Try not to use mass mailer attitude. You are sending your sales letter as a mass mailer. But the receiver might not appreciate that fact. The moment he sees that it is one of those bulk mail, he will throw it away.

Writing your letter with a "herd mentality" instead of focusing in on a single, individual prospect will really damage the chance of your letter to make a real link with the reader.

A sales letter is the only kind of marketing tool that is one-to-one. So make it as personal as possible.

Lethal Sales Letter Mistake # 2 - Do not write long boring letters. What in your opinion is a long letter? Even a one-page letter can seem to be long. This is so because it's not the length that is long, but the content of the letter.

People watch lengthy movies, read lengthy books and so on. But only if they are interesting. If you go on and on in a boring fashion, then chances are that you snugly go into the nearest bin.

Offer an appropriate product or service at a suitable price and present it in an interesting manner. Half the battle is won.

Deadly Sales Letter Mistake # 3 – Do not stick to only grammatically correct formal English. At school your teachers and professors were paid to correct your assignments according to the formal rules of grammar. But in reality, it's a different ballgame altogether.

You should write your letter in more "common" and informal parlance, to make it more user-friendly. You might have to break certain grammar rules. You might need to begin sentences with "and" or "but." You might have to use abbreviations and fragmented words. The basic objective of a sales letter is not to get grade A Grade but to generate sales.

Lethal Sales Letter Mistake # 4 – Do not permit the reader to make any excuse for not reading your letter. In reality, no one is interested who you are or what product and service you offer. They are interested only in how you can benefit them.

So you have to grab your share of attention in the first 20 seconds or even less. Start with a provocative sentence or slogan. Try to attack the emotions. Your aim should be to hold onto the attention of the prospect.

Lethal Sales Letter Mistake # 5 - Not properly establishing your credential.

The evidence you offer up in your sales letter to support your pedigree can take quite a few different forms. For example:

Put in testimonials of people who have used and gained from your product or service. Put it in the form of stories. To make your testimonials even more influential include pictures of your customers with their names, addresses, and phone numbers. Most readers won't call to find out. But if you include the numbers, it lends you greater credibility.

(h) What Are The Pitfalls Of A "What If" Approach?

"What if I could demonstrate how you could save money in spite of not cutting down your daily expense?"

"What if I tell you that you can enhance your market share in 3 months time?"

"What if I can make you lose weight in no time?"

Now what if you are a prospective consumer who has already heard these "phony" statements before. Do you at all think you will be motivated enough to buy?

Scheming selling practices are rarely successful when it comes to dealing with customer opposition, and they really have no position in the world of proficient selling.

The genuine method is to address your prospect's opposition during the sales process itself. This means soliciting the right questions early on and customizing your product or service to solve their problem.

It is true that many people will have objection to buying your stuff. The best way out of this condition is to inquire about their real needs, trying to gauge their trouble and offering them a product or service that will actually benefit them. And for that, you need to put in a good amount of time on them.

You need to ask first-rate questions that make your client think. This may sound very easy; but in reality, it is very complicated because challenging questions are hard to ask. Many sales people recognize these types of questions as personal and often imagine that their customers will not be enthusiastic to answer them.

What's significant to remember is that most people ask tough questions and as a consequence have slight or no uncertainty in responding to them. In fact, it will raise your position in their eyes.

You can ask questions like:

- What are your short-term goals?
- How do you intend to accomplish these objectives?
- What confrontations are you experiencing in reaching these objectives?

Your basic objective out of this conversation would be to find out what problem the prospect is facing and how you and your product or service can solve it.

Let's not run away from the truth. Buyers today are much more complicated than they were ever before, and in all probability, they have heard every line similar to whatever you want to say. And they loathe people who use clichéd and traditional lines or manipulative approaches.

Most people articulate certain objections about making a buying decision. Thus sales are closed because your buyer sees the worth in your product or service or because you have proved yourself as a specialist who can assist them resolve a problem.

Just asking "What if I could" is not a successful advance. It's clichéd and hardly works nowadays.

(i) What To Do When You Just Cannot Write A Sales Letter?

You require to carve out a sales letter, but you just can't find the words. You think and think and think but to no avail. So what do you do now?

It's a really exasperating situation and can happen to us all anytime. But there's a great way to make your creative juices flow out.

Ask questions

Are you really aware of your product?

Suppose you are selling a treadmill. You really need to know how it feels to use it. When can you use it? What are the limitations and side effects?

Knowing and caring about your product gives you the passion to tell the whole wide world about it. To praise it. To love it. To flaunt it.

So now the first block is overcome. Now that you know the product and fallen in love with it, you can blabber on to describe it.

Next, record the reasons why and how it'll help you, if at all. Will it make my life easier? Will it add value? Will it solve a problem? Also, is it too expensive? Is it too ugly, and so on.

List everything: the good, the bad, and even the ugly.

You need to find out the reason why people will buy from you at all.

What is so unique about your product or service? The best way to do this is to brainstorm.

Shortly, you'll have so many opinions hitting you that you will not be able to keep pace. Just continue the process till you have exhausted all ideas.

Once you are done, all you require to do is take a look at what you have penned down and make a list of all the spectacular ideas you have. List them in order of priority.

Now you have the rough draft for your letter.

Utilize the most significant basis on the list, the main motive why someone should buy your product, and turn this into a marvelous headline.

Permit the ideas on the list to pour into your sales letter using sub-headlines or highlights when you need to stress a point. Soon, your letter will have almost written itself.

In conclusion, when you write your letter, keep in mind to write it to only one individual at a time. Make it special!

(j) The Disparity Between A Sales Letter And An Advertisement

People often get the conditions ad and sales letter confused. Both are intended to get new targets or sell a product or service. But there are significant differences in how they act.

A sales letter is a more individual form of advertising than any advertisement. Thousands or perhaps millions of readers will witness an ad in a magazine or newspaper. A sales letter is for the intended reader's eyes only. Even though sales letters are often printed in bulk, the reader still considers the mail as more personal than an advertisement in a newspaper or magazine.

Unlike an advertisement, a sales letter is more personal, informal, and warm. This conveys a more informal and natural tone. In this manner, the reader gets a better feel of the writer's character, interest, and seriousness.

(k) Attention Is Critical

For any marketer, attention is a prized product. With consumers bombarded with thousands of advertising letters each day, the challenge is how to make your message stand out of the crowd becomes even more serious.

Any winning sales letter must achieve two things:

1. It must make the prospect read through the whole letter.

2. It must prompt the prospect to carry out the desired action.

If the marketer failed to achieve Step 1, Step 2 is impossible.

Many marketers try to make the envelope very attractive. They know that their battle is half won if they can make the prospect open the letter.

For online marketers, there is no prospect of an envelope. Certain webmasters create flash images to attract readers.

Tips to grab attention:

1. Quite a few tests have shown that a RED headline gets noticed over any other font color choice. The color red is often related with danger, but it also signifies, "This is significant. Read me!"

2. Get rid of anything from the page that doesn't hold up the sales message or distracts from it. This comprises most animated graphics and intense colors for the page backdrop that contends with the foreground text. Nothing strikes just simple black font alongside a white background. If you can restrain the number of colors used to three or maybe less, this will also help in making the document reader friendly.

3. Do not make the text too wide, as it becomes monotonous to read from a single line to the next because too much head and eye movement is required.

4. The headline must be catchy and interesting and should jump out at you.

5. The format and design of the sales letter should be appealing to read. Suitable highlighting, bolding, bulleting and subheads all make the letter simple to read.

6. Make the letter very inviting and appealing.

7. The letter should prompt the user to keep reading. You need to go on nudging the prospect to read further.

8. Be EXCLUSIVE. If all of the sales letters in your sector look and read identical, then why should a prospect read yours? You can use mascots, humor, cartoons, and so on.

9. Focus your message on the reader, not on your organization or product. This is a chief collapse of big businesses who think that everyone should just be familiar with how great their corporations are. But your prospect is essentially inspired by selfish desires. He needs to know what is in it for him.

(l) A Rapid Lesson In Writing Sales Letters In A Lucid Manner

What kind of sales letter gets read? What kind of sales letter enhances selling? What kind of sales letter keeps the reader's interest intact till the last word?

I would say that it has to do with the "conversational tone" of the sales letter. You feel that you are at home with a good friend who is giving you some advice over a refreshing drink and snacks. You are relaxed and comfortable.

So how do you generate a conversational tone?

1) Use succinct sentences. When you talk to a friend, you talk in phrases. You do not use long, winding, and difficult jargon-filled sentences.

2) Use descriptive word pictures. Use words that will create an image in your mind. Describe it thoroughly. Create an image.

3) Write whatever comes from your heart. Do you edit when you talk to your friend? Rarely. Similarly, keep writing whatever comes from your heart.

4) Talk to your prospect in her own language. Mention something she can identify with, that is not in professional parlance.

Just give it an attempt and see the change.

A few tips to format your sales letter for improvement

1. The headline should be catchy and at the apex of the page so that the reader can view it without scrolling.
2. The finest color to use for the headline is RED.
3. Insert your name near the top of the page and before the body of the "sales" text and also at the bottom of the "sales" text.
4. Scan your real signature and insert it.

5. Use sub-headlines.
6. Sub-headlines should be the identical color as your main headline, RED.
7. Draw interest to your testimonials by inscribing them in separate boxes. You can also use a separate color for the box.
8. A good testimonial should state specifically what the satisfied customer liked about your product, service, etc. Highlight the specific thing that person liked.
9. Try avoiding putting the price in red, as red would mean stop. It may be good for the headline, but it is not for the price.
10. Bonuses should relate to your offer.
11. Highlight important parts of your sales letter.
12. Use a payment method that has some credibility and acceptance, and even better, include several different payment methods.
13. Just like they work on paper, sticky notes on your website encapsulate your visitors' attention for a few seconds. See that those seconds work for you.
14. Use white space to give a break in the clutter. Give the eye rest.
15. The font and color chosen should be readable and attractive.
16. A sales letter should always use a call to action. Specify how you want your prospect to act. Don't presume that he will know.

(m) What Is Better - A Long Or A Short Sales Letter

Does a long sales letter generate sales or a short one? In actual fact, long or short is relative. The basic objective is to be interesting. If the sales letter is interesting, then it can sell your product or service irrespective of the fact that it is in one page or 24 pages.

It has been noticed that a long, interesting sales letter constantly translates more prospects into buying customers.

Why is this so? A long and interesting sales letter makes the reader feel at home with a friend. It evokes a feeling of companionship, which deepens as the letter proceeds. It talks to you as if it knows you and cares for you. It creates a bond.

Your letter has to identify with your prospects and try to know their real needs. The letter should make them feel that you empathize with the reader and realize his problem. It should make them feel that yes, you do care.

This creates a sense of trust. The prospect feels that you surely understand his problems and keenly awaits your solution.

Your letter should be customized for each prospect. Avoid the "crowd mentality."

Faith is the most significant emotion that you need to win. Once your prospects start trusting you, they will not only purchase your product or service but happily recommend it to others. Grape vine or word of mouth is yet another valuable marketing tool.

So use long interesting copy for your sales letter.

(n) Do You Always Have To Use Correct English

Many copywriters believe that they always have to use correct spellings and astute English when they write a sales letter. However it is not always the case. Copywriting has got very little to do with "actual writing."

Only a mere portion of the whole letter involves "actual writing." It is basically how you format it and how you present information to your prospective client.

For example: What if I sent you a letter that was typed with an aged, broken up word processor, with all kinds of grammatical mistakes. And the letter said, behind all these typo errors, I have chosen you through a lottery to give you a billion dollars as a windfall gain. Do you care about the errors and spelling mistakes? No. You are now on Cloud Nine with joy.

On the other hand, assume that I type out a perfect letter on the best quality paper. No spelling or grammatical errors. I also spray in some perfume. But at the end of it I am trying my best to sell you an old dilapidated building in the outskirts. Now do you care? Oh, no.

It's not how you articulate it that really matters, it's what you state.

The bottom line is: There can be exceptions to this, but the truth remains that if you focus on distributing your proposals to people who have already shown that they are interested in products or services similar to yours with a truly irresistible offer, your chances of bagging the deal are far higher than if you just approach semi- or non-interested people with a perfectly written sales letter.

(o) Monster Of A Sales Letter

More often than not, marketers produce their own monsters (just like Dr. Frankenstein) in their sales letters.

Sales letters work best when you have something to sell. It basically boils down to responses like this: What exactly can you do for me? Why do you think I should spend my valuable time reading any of your letters? Quick... convince me that I need the product or service which you are offering me.

When creating a better sales letter, start off and instead of using the wrong head like our Dr. Frankenstein, use the right HEAD.

The right head can create or smash your sales letter. Focus it firmly on your target market. Tackle a big problem your target confronts (presuming you have the answer to it). If you can do this by intelligently playing with words, then certainly go for it; but if wordplay isn't your cup of tea, keep it simple and uncomplicated. There's no perfect measurement lengthwise for a headline, but don't misuse words. Keep it to one sentence. The purpose is, make them think about you.

Once you've hooked them with your headline, don't let them run away. As we have already seen, P.S. is one of the most important parts of your letter. So don't waste your P.S. on useless words.

Say something that will cheer your reader to go back to the beginning of the letter and continue reading.

The first paragraph is also very important, so get straight to the point. Show them the crux of your offer. Let them know what fortune they will make or how comfortable their life will become or how convenient the offer is and so on.

If you can involve and interest the reader by your first paragraph, let the rest of the letter answer the basic questions and speak to them about the general worries your reader may have. Since you have worked so hard, it will be such a disgrace to lose them on technical issues.

Fill the body of your letter with benefits, not just features. Your benefits and features must be able to solve all the "So what?" and "why you?" tests.

Talk to your target in their lingo. Write informally. Ask questions and answer them. Create as lucid a letter as you can. Use humor as much as you want, but be careful that it does not misfire. The readers should not misunderstand your intentions in any way.

Every one is hard-pressed for time. But what can you do? You have to get to them in the midst of this only. Use bold and highlights to mark certain information. This will catch the readers' attention and encourage them to go on reading.

Now you have gone on about how good your product and services are. But why should they believe you? So now what do you do? Simple. Include some testimonials of satisfied clients. Let them tell your prospects how good your products or services are. Testimonials are influential selling tools that establish your claims to be true.

Once you've addressed all the possible doubts and questions in the body, it's time to put your best foot forward again. Go over your offer. And, if you can, offer a guarantee of fulfillment. When you offer a guarantee, you diminish the cynicism around the purchase of your product or service. Consumers are reasonably careful and more so when making purchases via the Web. And guarantees give you an almost immediate trustworthiness with possible customers. Guarantees increase perceived value.

Once you have completed the letter, forget about it for sometime. This will allow you to be more practical when you edit your letter.

Before sending out your mailer, always test the market. Fine-tune it according to your reaction. Then go on to track your responses to extra fine-tune both the letter and your target market.

A sales letter will never achieve all of your expectations. Carry on with your other marketing endeavors, and don't forget to rapidly follow up on all leads created by your sales letter.

Put it together with care and dexterity. A good sales letter forces your audience to make a favorable response toward you.

Your business printer can help you tactically build up a variable printing campaign that takes the benefit of personalization. Here you must realize the value of good printing. That is to say, using a good-quality printer and paper. Although the real cost of every mailing will be superior, the better return of each mailing at all times creates a higher return on investment. The bottom line is that good business printers can assist you arrive at your sales expansion targets quite easily.

Create a proper budget. See if you can control costs in some other fashion. But do not try to use low-quality paper and ink. That degrades the reader's impression. What basically matters is the content of the sales letter and not the glitter outside. Similarly, it is also true that a good glossy paper and shiny ink will definitely enhance your prospective client's chance of reading the letter.

(p) Is It True That Good Sales Letters Are Like Good Sales People?

Find out for yourselves. To begin with, you should compare them with newspaper advertisements put up for salespeople. The qualities employers look for in a salesperson, you should look for the same in a sales letter.

1. Is he a Self-starter?
The best salespeople need the slightest amount of direction. They are self-inspired. Similarly, your sales letter needs to work on its own. If you want your prospect to buy on the basis of the letter, your sales letter must give each benefit, feature, selling promise, proof, and guarantee that is needed to close the sale.

2. Does he have prior experience?
The best sales people find out from their blunders. So should your sales letters. The letter you are about to mail needs to be tested to make certain your list, your offer, your imagination, and your timing is the best they can be.

3. Does he work well under pressure?
Your prospect is engaged and unfocused. Your letter will in all probability arrive as a disruption. So make sure your letter works hard to grasp the concentration of your probable buyer and make your sales pitch.

4. Does he have excellent communication skills?
Make sure your sales letters are simple and user friendly. It should speak in the general language of the people.

5. Is he energetic?
Your sales letters need to have a clear vivacity to them.

6. Does he have proven organization skills?
A sales letter should be organized and disciplined.

7. Is he a team player?

Occasionally, your sales letter will not be able to work on its own. If your letter is intended to create a lead and not make a transaction, for example, it likely has other group players like print ads, telemarketing, hoardings and so on) that it must work with to arrive at the required target.

You need to make sure that the pitch of the sales letter is at par with the other marketing tools.

8. Does he have excellent customer service skills?

It is true that sales letters are a one-way conversation, but you can compose them to seem more like a two-way talk can't you? The more that your letters evoke a warm, human, and real tone, the better.

9. Only serious candidates should apply

Prepare and mail a sales letter only when you are serious about offering a promise and keeping it.

10. Like a good salesperson, a good sales letter should always ask closed-ended questions, since these permit you to get specific answers and move toward concluding the sale. Closed-ended questions begin with verbs, for example "Are," "Will," "Is," "Have," "Did," "Aren't," "Didn't," and "Won't." It is answered with a "Yes" or a "No." You usually employ this technique when you want to start tapering the conversation and getting precise answers that will lead you to close the deal.

You can also ask more specific questions like, "Do you realize that you have __ problem?" or "Will you make this decision in a fortnight's time?" "Do you like my product or service?" "Would you like to begin on it right away?" "Are you happy with your existing supplier?" Such questions force the prospect to make a decision.

You must always ask closed-ended questions in an affectionate, friendly, inquisitive tone of voice. Always be well mannered and kind. You should never use force or exploitation. It never works. On the contrary, it works against your cause. You lose credibility.

(q) The Ten Basic Rules Of Writing A Good Sales Letter

For many small enterprises, a sales letter is the only marketing tool. They might not have a budget for anything else. But a carefully mapped out sales letter can create magic for your top line and bottom line. Just follow a few guidelines as mentioned below and see your profits soar.

- **You must always target the wants, needs, and desires of your prospective clients.** Walk a mile in the prospect's shoes before writing any sales letter. Remember what they are looking for in the letter is "What exactly is in it for me?" So tell them what is there for them.

- **Avoid the crowd mentality. Write to specific people.** You should write to a real and living person. Write the letter as if you're writing to one friend, not to 1000's of people.

- **People buy benefits and not features.** You should begin by distinguishing the benefits from the features. The sales letter should be able to influence your reader to buy your stuff based on the grounds of what benefit the product/ service derives and not based on its features. It is the benefit the buyers buy and not just the feature in isolation.

- **Hook your readers with the first line itself.** You have to compete with several unsolicited mails at any given time. So your letter should be crisp and catchy. The headline should make the reader read the first line, the first line should make him read the second, and so on.

- **Provide the reader with specific and relevant information.** Do not go on and on about a product or service. Do not go around in circles. List specific benefits and tell them how their life would be easier with the benefits that are being offered.

- **Your sales letter must sell.** The basic aim of your sales letter is to sell, isn't it? It must sell. And for it to sell, it must be written in a conversational tone. Talk to your prospect in a lucid and friendly manner. Chuck the ornamental language and think of basic grammar rules as optional.

- **Test your sales letter.** Try and ask yourself, if someone was writing the same letter to you, would you get convinced enough to spend your hard-earned dollars on it?

- **Make the sales letter as lengthy as it has to be.** There is nothing called too long or too short. The basic thing that matters is the interest factor. The sales letter should be interesting and appealing.

- **Focus on the aesthetics.** Use user-friendly fonts and templates that will make it visually appealing. You can use bullets and highlighters to break the clutter. Try not to end any page except the last page in a complete sentence. Most newspapers apply this tactic. If you do not end the page in a complete sentence, the reader will automatically navigate to the next page for completion.

- **Tell the reader precisely what to do.** What do you want the reader to do next? Does he have to send in a reply card? Or does he have to place an order? Or call for more information? Schedule an appointment? Notify him accordingly. Do not presume he would know. It is amazing how many sales letters fail to inform the reader about the subsequent step. They consider that the reader to be a mind reader. But sadly enough, this is not the case.

(r) Five Useful Secrets Of An Effective Sales Letter

The difference between an average sales letter and an effective sales letter is the result it derives. As already explained so far, it is not too difficult to write a million-dollar sales letter. You just need to follow a few tips and guidelines.

Here are five more insider secrets for writing a "killer" sales letter.

1. Spend a few hours each day by going through some of the most effective sales letters of all time. Try to learn the nuances. Try to see how they use the headline, how the lead paragraph is constructed. Look at the style, the structure, and so on.

2. You should also amass all of the best sales letters you find and generate a notebook out of them. Afterwards, when you sit down to write a sales letter, you can flip through your notebook of sales letters to get ideas for your project. Do not copy these letters. This would be considered plagiarism. Just pick out the basic ideas and put it all in your own words.

3. Research your prospective targets till you know everything about them. You must realize their wants, their desires, their dreams, and their aspirations. You must know what motivates them and what does not. Once you know that, it will be far more easier for you to write a sales letter that will have some positive effect on them. Your letters need to be personalized.

4. After you research your prospect, learn to relax. Once you have completed your investigation of the customer, forget about it all for a day or two. This will allow you to be more practical when you start writing your letter.

5. There is only one way you can ever find out if a sales letter will be winning or not. It has to be undergo a test. You have to send it out to a number of your potential prospects to see if it makes progress or not. If yes, then great. If not, you need to again go back to square one and put your brains to work.

(s) Do Emotionally Charged Sales Letters Boost Sales

Are you upset that your sales letter isn't receiving proper outcomes? Are you at your wit's end on how to boost sales via your sales letter?

If the answer to the above questions is in the assertive, then I would suggest that the solution to your dreary results is included in one single yet powerful word - Emotion. As you may have by now realized, buying judgments are found on the basis of emotion the sales letter must build on the reader's sentiment to a position where they are motivated to take action. The letter should try to attack those "hot buttons" or emotional pressure points, which will persuade the reader to buy. The main two motivating factors are the promise of gain and the fear of loss.

So how do you insert more emotion into your sales letters and thus charge up the selling ability of your copy? Here are a few examples.

1) **Agitate Ache**: Try to get inside the head of the reader. Focus on the problem the reader has. Point out to them how because of this problem, they're stalled, irritated, worried, and unable to achieve their sincere needs. You need to stir up their apparent problem and make it appear better than it actually is.

2) **Attention-grabbing Tales**: Stories are wildly successful in appealing to emotion. Watch a catastrophe, you'll feel miserable. Watch a sci-fi movie, and you'll almost certainly feel thrill.

Watch a horror flick, and you'll feel frightened. So interlace stories into your letters that awaken expectation in accomplishing a goal, avoiding difficulty, or attaining an aspiration. You can also include stories on what happened to someone who did not try out your product in solving their problem. This kind of story will create the dread of loss, which is more compelling than want to gain in most people. Tell a story about someone whom your readers can with no trouble connect to.

3) Use Emotion and not Logic: It's true that a number of words blaze stronger sentiments than others. You want to assess your target marketplace and discover what keywords your prospects actually respond to. The important thing to keep in mind is that almost every single word has an emotional ingredient to it. If your proposal is gain-oriented, then words and phrases like "money"; "get rich fast"; "million dollars"; and "earn from home" will stimulate your readers. Choose five or six keywords that'll swirl up the emotion you want in your reader and delicately place them throughout the sales copy to flash an emotional response.

As I have already said, there are innumerous ways to inject emotion into your sales letter. There are a multitude of emotions. You surely cannot put all these emotions in your sales letter. Most sales letters aim at one or two main emotions and then appeal to a few more. The more sentiments you can merge into your copy, the more commanding your letter will be.

Your sales letter should methodically explain the benefits of your product or service. Simultaneously, your product or service should resolve a quandary that your probable clients have stumbled on. In reality, any winning sales letter will have to accomplish an authentic need.

The appropriate sales letter should acquire trust from the very beginning and tell a motivating tale all throughout. This is not an assurance of an instantaneous sale but the start of an association, built on trustworthiness.

Of course, you have to apply emotion morally and sensibly. If you plan to apply it, think for a while and ask yourself how you would react if someone else aimed that kind of communication to you. This will assist you in deciding on your course of action. Test marketing at every phase is important for writing that "perfect" sales letter.

(t) What Are The Words That You Should Never Make Use Of In A Sales Letter?

There can be times, when no matter how many sales proposals you mail, the effect is nil. Do you know precisely why people don't seem eager to buy your product? Have you ever marveled why your opponents make more sales even though they have an awful product to offer?

You may feel that people are just plain uninterested in buying your product or service. You may also feel that your price is on the higher side. Or worse still, you may feel that you have a useless product or service and decide to quit altogether or maybe change your line of business.

Here you must stop and think for a while. Is it maybe not your product that is responsible? At times it's your own sales letter that turns out to be the main culprit. Maybe unwittingly you have used certain words which have had the opposite effect on your prospect.

So, what are precisely those bad or evil words you should in no way utter in your sales letter?

1) **Buy.** Never solicit people to take out their purse and pay out their hard earned dollars. Keep in mind, most people get wary the moment they see this word. Whatever business you're doing, using this word can obliterate your business in no time. Instead of using the word "buy," modify it to "receive" or "invest."

2) **Learn.** This term is sure to remind people of the old days, when they had to study and learn in school. Believe me nobody is interested in wracking their brains as they did when they were students. These days, people want quick information and have no time to learn. It is better to use the word "find out" Instead of "learn".

3) **Tell.** People will not pay attention to you if they don't identify you. Examine these two sentences carefully: "Let me just tell you how you can lose weight in one week" and "Let me disclose to you how you can lose weight in one week." Which statement do you think that will make an impact?

4) **Things.** Using this word will make your sales letter very dull and boring to read. As a substitute of using the word "things," consider changing it to "tips," "tricks" or "techniques." Trust me, this will guarantee a better and more open frame of mind.

5) **Stuff.** This is the word that most marketers use to explain how great the product is. Compare these two sentences: "Call us to receive fabulous stuffs" and "Call us to receive fabulous gifts." Which one do you think would generate more response?

Every sales letter has a set of vocabulary that is destined to activate the emotional buying spark within you. This language has to be cautiously assessed.

Appraise carefully; in the sales letter selling you some get-rich-quick ventures, you will encounter the use of certain words such as "**turn-key**." This entails that the business that they are asking you to join is all set to run, and that no or negligible work is necessary on your part to make a profit. But more often than not, this word in the sales letter is used to explain software that you still need to install, learn and work with to appreciate the service or product you are being provided. This is not right.

Be very aware of the word "**could**" and "**immediately get rich**." You could earn up to $100 to $1000 monthly. Assess what is the normal earning for someone who joins your affiliate program. Do not try to mislead or bluff. Though these words generate immediate response, you must use it only if you mean it. Remember there is absolutely no shortcut to success. So do not try it.

The success of any sales letter depends mostly on the words you use and how you craft them to serve your purpose. Once again, you do not have to be an

English scholar to dole out an effective sales letter; you just need to write simple English in a friendly and conversational tone.

(u) Ways To Create Rapport

Here are a few methods for creating rapport:

- In sales letters, we can frequently include a few statements that are clear yes questions.
  For example:
  > You realize how significant this is for you, don't you?
  > Don't you deserve the best?
  > Isn't this the best time to start it?

  > Adding a question mark as contrasting to a full stop is still open for discussion, so use what you feel will be finest for your circumstances. Your objective is to make your prospect agree with you and do what you say. Play on their emotions.

- Another method is analogous to the above-mentioned technique. You can include testimonials from satisfied customers. They are very useful in enhancing the perceived value. But use genuine testimonials. Do not try to bluff.

Mirroring is another method where you become like your prospects in appearance, tone, and jargon that they're well known with. For example, you will not talk to a doctor, as you will to an accountant or event manager.

Rapport is very alike to building credibility. The major dissimilarity between projecting an image of credibility and building a bond is that your prospect may trust you and yet she is not open enough to spend her hard-earned cash on your product or service. The basic fact is people have faith in those who are more like them.

Chapter 4 - Finishing Up

(a) Final Checklist for a sales letter.

- It is better to use the prospect's name and title.

- Try to make the sales letter user-friendly and special.

- Use anecdotes and slogans and catchy headlines

- Try to write like you generally talk. Read your first draft aloud to see if it has a lucid and free flow of words.

- Keep your paragraphs concise and use uncomplicated language. Speak in their lingo.

- Once you have completed the letter, forget about it for sometime. This will help you to be more practical when you edit your letter.

- Ask for criticisms and comments from friends and relatives about your sales letters.

- While keeping to a standard format, opt for something eye-catching like brightly colored paper.

- Use a user-friendly font.

- Always use P.S. or P.P.S. to attract attention.

- Use testimonials whenever available to enhance your credibility.

- Give a genuine and irresistible offer.

- Send out a few reminder letters.

- Give an "act now" option in terms of deadlines, free offers, limited stocks, and so on.

- Tell them what to do next. Don't presume your prospects know it for sure.

- Make your sales letter forceful, thrilling, and appealing.

- Use provocative and catchy slogans, something that attracts.

- Whenever possible, try to give a money-back or satisfaction guarantee.

- Include a reply card, phone number, and /or URL.

- Keep it short and sweet, precise and succinct.

- When you make your letter uneven, it is more probable to be opened, as it would have added to the curiosity factor. You can use rubber bands, cotton balls and other spongy things to make mail bumpy from the inside

- You can enhance readership when you hand-address each envelope. But see if your budget permits that. If not, do not overstretch.

- Don't distinguish your envelope with a business logo because it diminishes the ratio of openings.

Businesses are forever looking for ways to improve their marketing results, and this necessitates a more customized targeted method. A well-written and targeted sales letter will go a very long way toward enhance your sales value. If you can make the prospect feel that you really empathize with him and genuinely want to solve his problem, then almost the whole battle is won. You just require to follow a few tips and templates to craft out a spectacular sales letter that will solve your purpose.

(b) The Last Word

By now, you are conversant with all the aspects of crafting out a good sales letter. Let's just flip over a few basic parameters of any effective sales letter.

1. A sales letter, to be effective, should create hope. People today are always hard-pressed for time. Thus, they are all the time looking for products and services that will make their life convenient and comfortable. So keep inspiring hope.

2. Create a sense of urgency. To stimulate people to take action, you need to add incentives to the offer. You can create a sense of scarcity by informing your reader that either the stock is in limited supply or that your existing offer is valid for only a limited time period.

3. Appear as an authority on the subject. If you manage to do so, no matter what you are selling, they are going to be much more likely to buy what you have to sell. Chalk out your sales letter in such a method as to set up the belief that you are only trying to help people and that you do not really benefit from the sale.

4. Pretend to be unbiased while writing your sales letter. People hate to be cornered into buying by salespeople. They feel cheated even if, in actuality, they are not. So if your sales letter manages to convince them that your basic intention is just to help them find out what they require and how to go about the process, your job is almost done. You can expect them to unfasten up their wallets to you.

5. Persuade fear in your prospect. This is the strongest emotion you can use to your advantage. Try to get inside the head of the reader. Focus on the problem the reader has. Point out to them how because of this problem, they're stalled, irritated, worried, and unable to achieve their sincere needs. You need to stir up their apparent problem and make it appear better than it actually is. Then

tell them how they can fall into trouble if they did not take any action against it. And then, go about showing them how your product or service will help them overcome the problem.

6. Try to be different. You have to distinguish yourself from the crowd. Or else, why should anyone buy from you? The best way, maybe, is to tell your prospects not to buy the product or service you are selling them. Yes, it mind sound very foolish, but it is not. Tell your readers to go and buy the products and services offered by your competitors. Only when they are not satisfied with what they have to offer, they should try your products or services.

Successful sales letter writing expertise is crucial for the web business owner or entrepreneur. Profits are made and lost on the basis of sales letter writing. No matter how wonderful your product, if you cannot communicate that to your probable buyers, and convince them to buy your product, you will not make it. So learn to articulate the benefits of your products or services.

You don't have to be a spectacular writer to create sales letter that work. All you need to know is how to sell to people. You need to get under your prospective buyer's skin and train yourself to think like him.

Now you know the rules of the game. Put these tips and guidelines to work, and your sales letter is sure to have a relaxed and easy flow that will keep your prospects reading and eventually create profits for you.

www.ingramcontent.com/pod-product-compliance
Lightning Source LLC
LaVergne TN
LVHW020434080526
838202LV00055B/5177